THE
30-SECOND

IMPACT
RÉSUMÉ

MARTIN DARKE

THE 30-SECOND IMPACT RÉSUMÉ

Wilkinson Publishing Pty Ltd
ACN 006 042 173
Level 4, 2 Collins Street
Melbourne, Vic 3000
Tel: 03 9654 5446
www.wilkinsonpublishing.com.au
Copyright © 2011 Martin Darke

All rights reserved. No part of this publication may be reproduced, stored in a retrieval system or transmitted in any form by any means without the prior permission of the copyright owner. Enquiries should be made to the publisher.

Every effort has been made to ensure that this book is free from error or omissions. However, the Publisher, the Author, the Editor or their respective employees or agents, shall not accept responsibility for injury, loss or damage occasioned to any person acting or refraining from action as a result of material in this book whether or not such injury, loss or damage is in any way due to any negligent act or omission, breach of duty or default on the part of the Publisher, the Author, the Editor, or their respective employees or agents.

The Author, the Publisher, the Editor and their respective employees or agents do not accept any responsibility for the actions of any person - actions which are related in any way to information contained in this book.

National Library of Australia Cataloguing-in-Publication data:

Author: Darke, Martin.

Title: The 30-second impact résumé / Martin Darke.

ISBN: 9781921804434 (pbk.)

Subjects: Résumés (Employment)

Dewey Number: 650.142
Layout Design: Chris Georgiou
Cover Design: Jo Hunt

CONTENTS

FOREWORD

Whenever I think of Martin Darke, up pops a picture in my mind of a man who embodies positiveness and the sort of can-do attitude that we all need, at whatever age, whether we're looking for a job or not.

As you work through this remarkably practical and inspiring guide, you'll notice that positive attitude shining through, encouraging you to make the most of who you are and of your unique brand of skills and experience.

Whether you're out of work or looking for a new job, it's hard at times to retain that positiveness and belief in your own value and experience, but don't ever lose sight of who you really are. Work with Martin's résumé guide, use the document format and you'll be giving yourself the best chance possible of marketing yourself into the job that's right for you.

You'll also realise, as you do the work of analysing your experience and achievements along the lines Martin recommends, that you have something of real value to offer any sensible employer! So make sure you make the most of the assets you could bring to the job in the résumé and at interview.

Martin is in the rare position of knowing what he's talking about from both sides of the recruiter's desk; he's been on the wrong end of age discrimination when applying for jobs and he knows the process from the recruiter's point of view as well, from his years in executive recruitment. And he's built on both in recent years with his work counselling individuals on their job search direction and processes, at the same time as he prepares winning résumés for them.

Many people Australia-wide can directly attribute achieving their dream job to their wise choice of contacting Martin for help. Not only did he help them work through their job search dilemmas, but using the format laid out in this book, he prepared résumés for them that accurately reflected their skills, experience and potential.

There's no reason you can't do the same.

If it's a personal endorsement you want, I can say I know Martin's simple, marketing-focused résumé format works. I've used it to good effect myself as the basis of a consulting profile.

I've also introduced it, with significant success, to many of the mature-age jobseekers who have come my way via Working Connections, the job search service I have run for seniors' organisations for almost a decade.

So good luck and good job-hunting. And like Martin, stay positive and forget any notions of giving up!

Grace Johnston (www.busyboomers.com.au)
Aligning Your Work and Purpose (2000), You've Got the Job (2006), 101 Ways to Get a Job (2010).

INTRODUCTION

Over the years I've seen thousands of résumés in my work as a recruiter and as a businessman, and more recently as an employment consultant helping people with disabilities to find employment. I can quite honestly say that fewer than 10% of all these résumés actually did the owner any justice and presented them in their best light.

Frustrated jobseekers are too numerous to mention. Yet, with a little effort, all that frustration can be removed. Doors can once again be opened to interviews, and people can give themselves the chance to lead careers they want to lead.

By following the steps in this book you can easily develop your own high-impact résumé. It will be easy to read for the recruiter and potential employer. It will make you look good. It will make you feel good. It will help you to kick-start the next phase of your job search.

I remember a workshop I gave in Melbourne in 2001 to a group of mature unemployed people. After I had demonstrated this style of résumé and pointed out its obvious benefits, a gentleman towards the back of the room rose from his seat, explained that he had been made redundant some eight years ago and had struggled ever since, and then said, 'Why hasn't anyone shown this to me before?'

It was a good question. Why is it that job search agencies, career advisers and other professionals in this industry continue to use outdated material which is of little benefit to those that most need it, the jobseekers? I wish I knew.

You'll find this style of résumé very simple, but highly effective. It will significantly improve your chances of getting the interview. That's what résumés are all about, opening the door to an interview.

It works for anyone from a cleaner to a CEO, from sportspeople to ballet choreographers, from paramedics to teachers. In short, it works for everyone. You won't regret using it, not least because it will bring a smile to your face and make you believe that you are, after all, worth something.

Even better, once you've written your own, you'll want to write résumés for others. Go for it!

Martin Darke
www.a-new-career-direction.com

CHAPTER 1

RECRUITMENT –
WHAT'S IT ALL ABOUT?

Anyone interested in obtaining a job, and that makes not just millions of us but billions, will at some stage of their lives go through a recruitment process, except for the fortunate few who inherit the family business.

There are four main participants involved in the process. These are, in no particular order:
- Job seekers
- Employers
- Recruitment firms
- Résumé writers

Some would make a case for career advisers, career coaches, life coaches, psychometric testers and personality profilers, and those emerging companies who check the validity of qualifications and references. In some instances, even investigation companies play a part, but I prefer to concentrate on the process to which the vast majority of us will be exposed throughout our careers.

All job seekers need a résumé. There are many different styles, derived from many different sources. Your first introduction to a résumé will probably be through a career consultant at school or college, or it might be through a friend or relative. Then there are countless books, and now we have the Internet, with sites offering advice on not just résumés but cover letters and interview skills.

In local and national newspapers you will find advertisements by 'professional' (I use the term loosely) résumé writers, and the cost can range from very little to rather a lot. But why pay money (anything from $50 to $750) when so many websites offer free templates of résumés 'that work'? Where's the value?

How many résumé writers can't even spell the word 'résumé' properly? How many are using the résumé template provided in the word processing software on offer by one of the world's largest computer companies? What do computer companies know about writing résumés?

It is no wonder that job seekers are generally confused.

I've often read that, for a particular type of job, a job seeker needs a certain type of résumé. I think this is a MYTH. Who says? Why should one style hold sway over another and for what purpose?

I genuinely believe that there is no valid reason why résumés should not be standardised with a simple, easy-to-read format, which tells the reader everything they need to know in order to make the decision as to whether or not to interview the candidate.

I have used this style for golfers, nurses and doctors, paramedics, ballet choreographers, CEOs, cleaners, sales and marketing professionals, engineers, and many more. All of them got the interview.

After all, that's what résumés are for – getting the interview. So why shouldn't the playing field be level with everyone using a style which makes it easier for the employer or the recruiter to determine their interview shortlist from a whole bunch of applicants?

To me, everyone has potential, but it saddens me enormously when I come across individuals with something to offer who are frustrated that they cannot even get an interview. In the end, it simply comes down to the fact that they are not marketing themselves properly with their résumés, and in some cases they've paid hundreds of dollars for a so-called 'winning résumé'.

Everything to do with the recruitment industry is unregulated. There are no barriers to entry. Anyone can set up a recruitment firm, just as anyone can become a résumé writer. Interviewers, whether recruiters or human resource officers, are rarely trained in interview techniques.

The recruitment industry is driven by commission and short time frames. Recruiters are often young people with little work and life experience, and who are more adept at selling the service, usually by cold calling. More often than not, employers use recruiters to save themselves time. Driven by commission and the need to get the job done, recruiters tend to do things as quickly as possible. The sooner they provide the shortlist, the sooner the employer can conduct the interviews and select a candidate.

For employers who do not use recruitment firms, again it comes down to spending as little time as possible to find the right person because, in most cases, the recruitment exercise is driven by the resignation or dismissal of an employee and a replacement needing to be found to keep the organisation running properly.

Employers and recruiters, as part of the process of saving time, are going to spend very little time looking at résumés. This is widely recognised as a fact. You thus have 30 seconds to make an impact with your résumé. Of the many different styles available, the résumé which you will be introduced to in this book achieves that 30-second impact. Not only that, it can also act as a cover letter.

Everyone involved benefits. Employers and recruiters, because they save vital time in filling the vacancy; but most importantly YOU, because you are finally getting the recognition you deserve and significantly improving your chances of getting the interview, which is the first step towards obtaining a new job.

CHAPTER 2

WHAT DO COMPANIES AND ORGANISATIONS WANT?

Scan Internet job sites or the classified advertisements in newspapers nowadays and it seems that every organisation seeking new employees is 'dynamic' and offers 'exciting' roles with 'fantastic' career prospects. If ever there were adjectives which were overused, then these three have to be right up there. For most of us our everyday working lives are much more mundane.

However, whatever the nature of the organisation, you will always find that job advertisements refer to the need for particular skills and experience, and in some cases qualifications. For some of us this can be disconcerting, especially if we are entering the workforce for the first time.

Imagine yourself as a housewife who has devoted the past 15-20 years to bringing up a family, yet perceives herself as having little to offer to potential employers. Wrong! Raising children is one of the hardest jobs imaginable and calls for a raft of skills which need to be applied on a day-to-day basis.

So it's very possible, if our housewife 'packages' herself properly in a résumé, to demonstrate her potential to an employer.

That's just one example. In fact, anyone who packages themselves properly can easily stand out above the rest, but very few of us know how to do this.

How many of us have opted not to send in an application based on our perception that we don't meet an employer's expectations as outlined in the advertisement? Don't be put off so easily. Employers will always ask for the ultimate, but rarely will they achieve their aim, often having to compromise on an aspect of the chosen individual's background.

Remember too that you have no idea how many people will actually be applying, and if you are one of a few, and if the rest are using the same old tired format for their résumés, then you just might find yourself in the frame.

Certainly, if you opt to upgrade your résumé to the style in this book, then you will significantly improve your chances.

What else are employers looking for?

High on the list are ACHIEVEMENTS. Achievements demonstrate ability and application, as well as potential. Yet many jobseekers find it impossible to describe their achievements in their roles, simply resorting to a fairly meaningless list of responsibilities to flesh out their résumés. The longer the list, the better the applicant feels, but this is WRONG. The employer already has the job description. It's what you can bring to that job that counts, and sometimes it might simply be a better attitude than the previous incumbent.

Believe it or not, simply turning up on time every day is an achievement and of value, so with a bit of thought it is possible to find achievements in any job. For instance you might have:

- Delivered sales on target despite an economic downturn
- Introduced a new filing system which improved efficiency
- Saved $x by sourcing new suppliers
- Worked for 12 months without any sick leave

Next comes the need to know YOU. An employer or recruiter wants to know everything about you. In my opinion, there is no point trying to hide anything, except those things that have no real relevance. One of the biggest failings of recruiters and employers is that they often have misperceptions about people from reading their résumés. They ask questions such as 'I wonder if...?' or they jump to conclusions by saying 'It seems to me that...'. As a result, they move on to the next résumé, and they rarely go back to ones they've passed over.

So it's important to remove these misperceptions at their source by presenting the complete picture of you. Tell it like it is, even if there are one or two warts. If you get the interview, you'll know that the employer is genuinely interested. This also saves time, because if something is revealed at interview which automatically rules you out, then everyone's time has been wasted.

Of course, if you didn't get the interview, then tell yourself that if they didn't want you as you are, then it was never going to be the right match anyway. You are definitely not the loser.

There are certain things that employers want but they are not allowed to ask for. Many of these are covered by the term 'discrimination', and have no relevance to your ability to do the job. I'm one of thousands who has suffered from age discrimination, and with one major public-sector organisation I was rejected due to a slight infirmity (a bent arm due to an accident and subsequent operation) which would have had no effect whatsoever on my performance. I managed to get that ruling overturned after writing directly to the CEO. Looking back I should perhaps have taken the matter to a relevant tribunal.

It's a disturbing fact that discrimination still occurs and most organisations get away with it because it's a difficult, and potentially very costly, issue to prove.

Yet many individuals still make it easy for employers to discriminate. How? By including unnecessary items such as age, marital status, children and even religion on their résumés. There is NO requirement to do this, and your new résumé will not include any of these items.

With all this in mind, in the following chapters, we are going to break down each section of this style of résumé to help you understand how and why it's put together, and why it works.

But before we start composing the document, which is going to MARKET you in the best light, we need to look at three critical points which must be taken into account.

CHAPTER 3

THREE CRITICAL ELEMENTS

1. You have 30 seconds to make an impact

Confronted by a large number of applications, whether in hard copy or electronic format, a recruiter or potential employer is not going to take very long conducting the first sift, the purpose of which is to narrow the applicants down to those suitable for a first interview. It is widely accepted that the reader spends, at most, 30 seconds reading each résumé. Not very long, is it?

If you don't achieve that impact within those 30 seconds, then your résumé, the one you might have spent hours crafting to get it right, is consigned to the bin and often you don't even get an acknowledgement of your application.

So it's what you put in the top half of the first page of your résumé that counts. This is where you make your impact. Quite often the reader will not even have to turn the page. What they've read in this top half is sufficient to get you the interview. All of this is very achievable, as we will find out in subsequent chapters.

I'm assuming here that your résumé has made it through any electronic screening process that might have occurred. Some employers prefer to use software rather than human beings to conduct the first sift, word-recognition software which searches for keywords. Take it from me that your new résumé will include all those keywords, thus improving the chance of your résumé being seen by a real person.

2. An employer is NOT interested in your objectives

How often have I seen wishy-washy statements at the top of résumés along the lines of 'Looking to further my career with a company which values...' or 'Aiming to play a vital role in a team environment...'?

What do these statements mean? Where do they come from? Probably from an idealistic vision we all have of the perfect job with the perfect employer. Yet it is still all too common to see such objectives taking up unnecessary space and reducing the impact of the résumé.

Take it from me that an employer is NOT interested in your objectives. All they are interested in is filling the vacancy with the right person as quickly as possible.

I can think of only one possible exception to this rule, and this applies purely to people seeking their very first job. For instance, when a graduate is applying for an entry-level position with a firm and has a very clear idea of the potential, and how a career could progress, within that firm, such as a trainee accountant wanting to become a partner of an accounting firm. Or when a school leaver has a desire to work in retail or perhaps become an apprentice.

Even so, given the way that the workforce in modern economies has evolved and that attitudes towards 'careers' have changed so much, it is difficult to see the relevance of an objective in a résumé.

3. No more than two pages

I've reduced a 30-year career to one-and-a-half pages. The owner was very grateful. I've seen résumés over 10 pages long with the owner wondering why it was proving so difficult to get an interview. Sometimes the first few pages are taken up with personal details and meaningless lists of generic skills, those that everyone is expected to have, for instance 'interpersonal'.

What you did 10-15 years ago was just a stepping stone to where you are now, so there's no need to dwell on history, even more so if you've changed careers completely.

In exceptional circumstances, there may be something you did a long time ago that might be relevant to your present application. Include this, by all means, but bear in mind that employers look for recent experience unless you happen to be skilled in a profession where there is a genuine shortage of applicants.

Nothing puts recruiters off more than lots of pages of detail. What you've done in the past few years and what's relevant is all that matters to them. Generally speaking they look for round pegs to fit into round holes. By keeping your résumé short and succinct, you are doing them a favour, not forgetting yourself!

Having looked at what is of most importance to employers, and aware of the need for a 30-second impact, it's now time to start composing the document which is going to MARKET you in the best light.

We'll start with something very simple, which can cause problems – your NAME!

CHAPTER 4

WHAT'S IN A NAME?

My full name is Jason Martin Darke, yet I've always been known as Martin. It's a long story. Whilst Jason is a very common name nowadays, in my childhood it was extremely rare. Consequently, kids used to laugh at me and my name was always a stigma whenever I heard it mentioned. It has taken me years to accept, and I reckon now, should I ever become a film star, Jason Darke would be a fabulous name.

But that's beside the point. You will never see 'Jason' on my résumé, but not because of what you've read above.

When applying for a job, you are not applying for a passport or a driving licence. For these it's compulsory to provide your full name. But in applying for a job, use the name by which you want to be called. So if your name is 'Robert' but you prefer 'Bob', then use 'Bob'. Likewise for 'James' and 'Jim'. This also obviates the need to explain how you prefer to be addressed whenever a recruiter calls you to set up an interview.

In western countries this might seem a minor issue, but for foreign nationals from countries such as Thailand and India, their names can be an impediment, often extending to six or seven syllables. Sometimes recruiters might not even bother to call for fear of embarrassing themselves trying to pronounce names.

Imagine an executive narrowing down an interview shortlist to ten candidates, all with more or less the same credentials, and then telling his secretary to line up five for an interview. It's obvious which ones the secretary will call first if some candidates have unpronounceable names.

Should you be someone with a long name, if you haven't done so already, adopt an easily pronounceable short form of your name to make it easy for the recruiter or employer. You won't regret it!

One final point on names. Occasionally it is difficult to tell the gender of an individual, so the use of 'Mr' or 'Ms', in brackets, can easily overcome this issue should it ever arise. Of course we are assuming that discrimination will not take place as a result, but sometimes that risk has to be taken.

Your name is one part of your personal details. What else do you need?

Simple. All that's required are your contact details, namely:
• address
• telephone numbers
• email address

In most cases you won't even need to include your physical address as virtually all correspondence will take place by email, but it's probably wise to include this so that an employer can gauge where you live in relation to commuting time and the responsibilities of the job.

On the subject of email, ensure you have a 'sensible' address, as something like ilovebubbles@hotmail.com can create the wrong impression. Recently, when helping my own brother, a professional golfer, with his résumé, I came across an interesting example as he was using 'belliedwedge' for his email address. This conjured up all sorts of things in the imagination but it is in fact a golfing term.

In military terms, as far as personal details are concerned, name, rank and serial number just about sums things up or, in our terms, name, telephone number and email.

So forget marital status, children, health, driver's licence (unless actually required) and all those other things which recruiters might use to rule you out. They are not necessary.

Though it seems obvious, we've covered the vital first element of our new résumé, our personal details. The best part about this is that we've taken up only two or three lines at the top of the page Here's an example:

MARTIN DARKE
14 xxxx xxxx, Quinns Rocks WA 6030
Phone: (Home) (xx) xxxx xxxx   (Mobile) xxxx xxx xxx
Email: mdarke@abcnet.net.au

Let's now look at what comes underneath. This is the heading, and it describes you and how you stand out above the rest.

CHAPTER 5

HIT THEM BETWEEN THE EYES – THE IMPORTANCE OF THE HEADING

Now that the reader knows your name and contact details, it's time to tell them what you do or what you aspire to being. What's your preferred role? If you're applying for a job as a receptionist, use 'receptionist' as a heading. If you're a chemical engineer, use 'chemical engineer'. If you're a salesperson, you could use 'sales professional'.

Now put yourself back in the shoes of the recruiter. If they've advertised a job for a receptionist, they immediately start to think here's a valid candidate. You, as the applicant, have saved the recruiter valuable time as they haven't even had to turn the page, or pages, to find out what you do! All they've read is a few lines at the top of the first page.

What comes next is really going to zap the recruiter right between the eyes. You are going to tell them what makes you stand out from the rest through what I call QUALIFYING DESCRIPTORS. These have the effect of starting to make you a favourite for an interview.

Qualifying descriptors are highly effective, not only in making you stand out but also in providing more information in just a few words.

Here's one using the words written in a farewell card from the rest of the team for a lady who was moving to a new town:

RECEPTIONIST

"You have been the face of this office, always so bright & cheerful in the morning. No matter how tired & grumpy we all are you always seem to make us smile." Ex-colleague

That sent a very strong message and she soon found a new job.

Here are a few examples:

CALL CENTRE OPERATOR

Capable of turning irate clients into ones that recommend us!

PROJECT MANAGER, CONSTRUCTION ENGINEERING

Specialising in $multi-million infrastructure projects

MARKETING PROFESSIONAL

Planning + ideas + hard work = results

All of a sudden, you start to sound interesting, a cut above the rest. You are presenting yourself in a totally different manner to the rest of the applicants, and the recruiter is enticed just a little bit more into calling you for the interview.

Qualifying descriptors are highly effective, not only in making you stand out but also in providing more information in just a few words.

Here's another example:

QUALIFIED TRAINER

Consistently rated as excellent by students
Strong business and consulting background, supported by IT qualifications

Next, think how difficult it is for an unemployed person to find a job. If you were the recruiter, would you consider inviting this person in for an interview?

UNEMPLOYED BRICKLAYER

Can't wait to get started again. Try me – you won't regret it!

It presents a whole new image, doesn't it? Our perception is completely changed.

Take a look at some more examples:

STOREMAN & PICKER

Fast, accurate, perfect attendance record

VERSATILE ALL-ROUNDER

Five blokes for the price of one!

DRIVER

Small trucks and vans, accident-free record

PROCESS WORKER

Consistent record of exceeding targets in a shift

SIMPLY THE BEST MATURE-AGED EMPLOYEE IN TOWN

*Loyal, committed, perfect health, unique range of skills including
accounting and IT
Available part-time, full-time or contract*

CUSTOMER SERVICE SPECIALIST

*Exemplary face-to-face and telephone customer service skills
Available part-time or full-time*

RECORDS & DOCUMENT MANAGEMENT SPECIALIST

Developing, implementing and maintaining best-practice systems

TECHNICAL SERVICES MANAGER
Specialising in process improvements and the implementation of technology

COMMERCIALLY ASTUTE ADVANCED ENGINEER
Turning ideas into profitable ventures
Enhancing systems to increase efficiency and turnover,
and improve the bottom line

ADMINISTRATION OFFICER
Bringing order to chaos, with a personal and friendly touch
Setting the standard for others to follow

SENIOR OPERATING & MANAGEMENT EXECUTIVE
Providing leadership and management to enable an organisation to meet
its goals and objectives

CHEMICAL ENGINEERING STUDENT
Looking for work experience in my field
Strong work ethic, great computer skills, a real team player

SPANISH GRADUATE WITH COMMERCIAL INSTINCT
Seeking an entry-level position in investment banking
Well travelled, confident and client-focused

So start thinking about your qualifying descriptors. What's going to make you stand out from the rest? What do you put into your job which makes you effective in your role and makes you attractive to a new employer?

Even in just a few lines we've made a huge impact on the reader. It's all about marketing YOU. Now comes a slightly harder part; describing you, as you are now, and what you can bring to an organisation.

CHAPTER 6

TELL IT LIKE IT IS

Writing about yourself is never easy, so it might be a good idea to brainstorm with a couple of people you respect to help you put this together.

You need to describe yourself in five to seven lines – what you are, where you're at in your life, what you are good at and what you can bring to an organisation. As we saw in Chapter 3 it is not about your objectives, it is about your future employer's objectives. Why would they want to employ you above everyone else? If you rate yourself highly, say so. Don't be shy in coming forward. This statement will tempt an employer to invite you for an interview. Humour can also play a part (see Chapter 12)!

Recruiters and employers, much as we would prefer them not to, tend to have misperceptions. They read things in résumés which aren't actually there, sometimes looking for an excuse to shove you aside and move on to the next candidate. So DON'T give them this opportunity.

Tell it like it is. If you're changing career, tell them. If you've taken a year off to go travelling, tell them. If you're looking for a step up in your career, tell them. Being enthusiastic about yourself can create the right impression. There is nothing wrong with liking yourself.

What you are trying to do is give them the complete picture. You will be giving them far more information than your competitors for the job. On that basis they can make the decision as to whether to grant you an interview. If the answer is no, then at least we've removed the potential for wasting everyone's time at an interview, at which will be revealed a reason for rejecting you; a reason which could have been covered in your résumé.

If the answer is yes, then you're in with a real chance. The recruiter is genuinely interested in the real YOU, the one you have revealed in your résumé. Nobody's time will be wasted, and you'll already be starting to feel confident about the interview, having removed the fear of being asked the question you didn't want to answer, the one that would have knocked you out of contention.

Let's look at a few examples. Here's one from a person applying for an administration role.

Diverse experience, from single-handedly setting up and running a backpackers' hostel to counselling drug addicts and ex-offenders to get their lives back on track, has given me the confidence to take on any role involving high expectations from both my employer and its clients. Service delivery and attention to detail are my strengths, to which is added a friendly style backed up by considerable knowledge and understanding of client needs. If you're looking for someone who is committed to getting the job done to the highest standard, then you won't be disappointed.

Next is one of a well qualified engineer who was struggling to find a job. Maybe it was because he had a 14-page résumé and recruiters just couldn't work out what he was capable of doing. He found what he was looking for within two weeks of sending out his new two-page résumé.

Accomplished and highly qualified mechanical engineer with the ability to take an idea from the design stage, acquire funding for research and development, and manage the project through to production and commercialisation. Particularly adapted to working alongside entrepreneurs in SMEs in developing new products, eventually setting up in-house facilities or outsourcing manufacturing. Recently returned to Perth after a successful spell in the technology transfer division of an academic institution recognised for its achievements in this sector. Now looking to assist Western Australian companies expand their operations and develop domestic and overseas markets.

If you're a person entering the workforce for the first time, then this one might give you some inspiration. This lady had decided exactly what she wanted to do, had acquired the relevant qualification, and was determined to find the right role. She's now looking after the library of a large firm in the resources sector.

My passion for working in libraries stems from being a prolific reader and also from a year's volunteering. Now, with the kids grown up, it's time to develop my career in this field. I've acquired a relevant diploma and accumulated plenty of experience (and praise) contracting for public libraries, law and accounting firms, and government departments. A full-time position is my target. In return you'll get hard work, dedication and commitment and, above all, a job well done.

Here's one from an individual who was looking to move forward and take a step up to more responsibility, something he achieved within a month, and is now working in countries he'd never thought possible.

Having emigrated to Australia in the late 80s, following an early career in printing and retail management in Ireland, my desire to help others led to what has become a very satisfying career as a paramedic, initially in the city and country, and more recently in remote environments. My longer-term aim is to add value to an organisation's safety practices by becoming more involved in the OH&S sector through training and raising awareness. Linked to this is my study of the Indonesian language, enhancing my communication skills with local workforces in the region. Highly adaptable and independent, working in any developing nation has a lot of appeal.

Finally, the story of a lady who took a step backward in her career to provide her with financial stability.

By working as a cleaner on a remote site for two years I've achieved my goal of financial stability. But it's now time to return to what I excel at and what I really enjoy, working in an office with a team of people dedicated to providing efficient and first-class service to its customers, both internal and external. My experience in this field is extensive, from reception to administration to data entry, a true all-rounder in every sense, totally committed to doing a job well. With my advanced computer and excellent interpersonal skills, I can apply myself to anything, so why not give me a try?

As you can see from all of the above, they tell a story. So much can be said in less than eight lines and the reader gets a pretty full picture. It's important to give a sense of what you can bring to an organisation, something that will benefit your new employer.

So believe in yourself and TELL IT LIKE IT IS!

CHAPTER 7

COMPLETING THE 30-SECOND IMPACT

As part of every role, employers look for skills and expertise. These are what qualify you to perform the job, and they are normally listed in the advertisement for the job.

So what you need to do next, to complete your 30-second impact, is alert the employer to the fact that you have all the skills and expertise they are looking for.

It's a very simple procedure. You need to find nine items, under the heading of 'Areas of Expertise' or 'Skills & Attributes', and highlight them in bold type in three rows of three each.

Here's one relevant to the position of an assistant accountant.

AREAS OF EXPERTISE

FINANCIAL ACCOUNTING	RECONCILIATION	PROFIT & LOSS
SYSTEMS	PAYROLL	A/CS PAYABLE & RECEIVABLE
TAXATION	DATA ENTRY	ANALYSIS & REPORTING

The one below is for a marketing professional.

AREAS OF EXPERTISE

MARKETING	SALES	PROMOTIONS
STRATEGIC PLANNING	RELATIONSHIP MANAGEMENT	MARKET RESEARCH
PROJECT MANAGEMENT	BUSINESS DEVELOPMENT	DATA MANAGEMENT

Here's one for an office all-rounder.

SKILLS & ATTRIBUTES

CUSTOMER SERVICE	RECEPTION	DATA ENTRY
ADMINISTRATION	BUILDING RELATIONSHIPS	PAYROLL
COMPUTER LITERATE	SUPERVISOR	TEAM PLAYER

It's easy to see how this works. Study the job advertisement closely and identify the skills the employer requires. Pick out the first one and place it in the top left-hand corner of our grid. The second can be placed in the middle of the first row or column. It doesn't really matter as the employer starts to read from the left-hand side and immediately begins to think that the candidate has what it takes, notably all the skills the employer is looking for.

You can imagine the effect this has on the reader. 'Looks like a perfect candidate – everything we need – bring them in for an interview!'

The employer or recruiter has not even begun to read about your current position and what other jobs you've had in the past. It's a simple, highly effective style which really does work.

Bringing all the elements of Chapters 4-7 together in one example looks like this, your 30-second impact:

MARTIN DARKE

14 xxxx xxxxxxx, Quinns Rocks WA 6030
Phone: (Home) (xx) xxxx xxxx   (Mobile) xxxx xxx xxx
Email: jmd@bigpond.com.au

ADMINISTRATION OFFICER

Providing all-round support to enable executives to do what they do best
Setting the standard in dependability and efficiency

Highly professional, loyal and capable administrator who recognises that the customer comes first and that, unless systems are up to scratch, service levels will fall, hence the need to maintain and improve standards in order for the firm to remain competitive. Whilst I have enjoyed my role and achieved due recognition, it's time for a change of environment after seven years. My record speaks for itself. If you're looking for someone who is a real team player and will make a genuine contribution, you have nothing to lose by giving me a try.

SKILLS & ATTRIBUTES

CUSTOMER SERVICE	ADMINISTRATION	CORRESPONDENCE
RECORDS MANAGEMENT	DATA ENTRY	BUILDING RELATIONSHIPS
COMPUTER LITERACY	SYSTEMS	TEAM PLAYER

Concise, to-the-point, and a complete picture of the individual, all designed to make it very easy for the employer to make a decision about interviewing YOU! That's what we are trying to achieve, and in 30 seconds you've made a big impression, all within the top half of the first page.

From here it's now just a case of outlining your previous experience, along with some essential information under a few other headings.

CHAPTER 8

LAYING OUT YOUR PAST EXPERIENCE

A common deficiency in most people's résumés is that they fail to describe the nature of their current and previous organisations. For instance are they:

- a small local firm
- a branch office of a national company, or
- part of a multinational?

Are they public or private sector?

Do they have fewer than 10, 10-100, or more than 100 employees?

A recruiter cannot be expected to know the name and nature of every single organisation in the economy, so it is important to let them know, and this can easily be done in two lines in most cases.

Next, we need to pay attention to the roles you have played.

Your current job title is highly relevant, but what if you've been with the same firm for over ten years and have progressed through the ranks in several roles? Rather than list all of your previous positions it is much more effective to add a short sentence along the lines of 'Commenced as a trainee in sales administration and rose to my current role as Sales Manager through several promotions'. Any significant highlights and achievements from those previous roles can still be included.

There is no point dwelling on what you did more than ten years ago. It is what you are doing now that is relevant to the job you are applying for. If you can slip in the word 'promotion' then this creates a very favourable impression on the reader, and leads us on to our next topic which is important to this section.

In the event that your past few roles have been significant and need to be listed separately, say, for instance, if you had been transferred to different divisions within a conglomerate, then a simple explanatory heading (in italics) can save a lot of unnecessary text, e.g. *The next four positions, between 1996-2006, were all with subsidiaries of the same group, XYZ Ltd.*

Nowadays, prospective employers are looking for ACHIEVEMENTS. What did you contribute which makes you stand out from the rest? What can you bring which makes it worth their while employing you?

In listing past experience, most of us tend to concentrate on job responsibilities, repeating our job description as if the reader simply doesn't know what is involved in our role. This does not add any value as job descriptions are similar in most organisations.

So, in analysing your experience you need to describe some achievements. Examples might be:

- increased sales by 10% over three consecutive years
- cut costs by 5% by streamlining systems
- improved efficiency by re-allocating tasks
- introduced flexible working hours which improved staff morale

Language is important, especially the use of action verbs such as 'increased' or 'improved'. Refer to Appendix B for more action verbs.

Ideally you should not need more than four bullet points for each position, but you can extend to five or six in some cases.

What if you can't find any achievements? Turning up to work on time each day is an achievement, as is not taking any sick leave over an extended period. Working overtime to help your boss or your team meet their commitments demonstrates commitment, and again creates a good impression. However, if you really do find there is not much scope in this area, then list the three or four key aspects of your role.

Summarising all of the above, here's a few examples:

MARKETING EXECUTIVE
METAL GALVANIZERS (WA), Perth

April 2002 to Present

Part of Alpha Group Australia, with global associates, the Galvanizing Division has plants throughout Australia. Turnover in WA exceeds $10m with a total staff of around 40. Commenced as Marketing Coordinator and promoted within a year.

- Contributed to turning an annual $600,000 loss into a projected $800,000 profit
- Totally responsible for all internal and external sales functions
- Developed marketing material and organised various promotions
- Revamped systems for targeting customers and organising quotes

R&D ENGINEER
AERONAUTIC ENGINEERS, Paris

May 2004 to Present

Subsidiary of ABX, specialising in the design and manufacture of engine components and sub-assemblies for aircraft and rocket launchers.

- Development and implementation of new technologies to manufacture spherical parts for cryogenic valves
- Implementation of innovative and efficient surface control technologies based on surfometry and optical interferometry
- Trainer and supervisor of R&D engineering team in fluid mechanics, cryogenic sealing, mechanical design and tribology
- Approved problem solver on rocket engine test sites for valve technical issues

SHIFT SUPERVISOR
RTS FERTILISERS, Sydney

May 2001 to Dec 2005

Part of an international chemicals group employing some 8,100 people on more than 100 sites across 21 countries. The Sydney operation employs 150 staff and supplies fertilisers across Australia.

- Supervise team and delegate tasks, operating to company guidelines and safety procedures
- Monitored and reported dysfunctions, ensuring minimal downtime
- Ensured high degree of quality control and on-time delivery
- Kept accidents and injuries to a minimum by anticipating potential problems

CHAPTER 9

BUT WHAT ABOUT THOSE GAPS?

Employers and recruiters don't like to see gaps. They can't help it. It's their nature. Gaps prompt them to have misperceptions and look for ways to rule you out and move on to the next candidate.

We are all subject to periods in our lives when we are not in the workforce. This is perfectly normal. So the best thing to do is explain the gaps. Remove the misperceptions at source and let the recruiter decide for themselves, based on all the evidence, whether they want to meet you for an interview.

Consider these examples:

Having been made redundant by XYZ Ltd, I spent several months performing part-time and casual roles whilst searching for an appropriate full-time position.

Continued my further development through comprehensive project management training followed by MBA studies, financing these activities through various part-time roles.

Took a year off to move to China and immerse myself in the Mandarin language, in which I am now fluent.

Prior to commencing full-time employment, I had several part-time jobs conducting household market research for reputable research firms.

Spent this period acting as primary carer for my elderly and very sick father.

Each of the above is a simple explanation. The reader is left in no doubt about what was happening in your life. For those who become unemployed, the chances of finding a new job immediately are not always good, but at least you can say you were looking and keeping yourself busy in the meantime. It is unlikely that a recruiter is going to conduct an in-depth check into your activities during such a period.

What interests them is what you can bring to the organisation, your personality and where you're at right now in your life. In short, is there a fit?

DON'T LEAVE ANY GAPS!

CHAPTER 10

HOW FAR BACK DO I GO?

This is a very common question.

What you were doing 20 years ago is probably of very little relevance to the job you are applying for now. On the other hand, what you were doing then might be the starting point for the glittering career, in your chosen field, that you've enjoyed since.

However, unless there's a clear need or unless the recruiter actually demands a complete history, there really is no need to go back more than 15 years. Some people say 10 years.

Even then, whenever dates are included, the recruiter is bound to get a sense of your age and may well be using this to rule you out. Age discrimination is all too rife.

It is not a crime to leave out the early years of your career but if you do feel a sense of duty towards your potential future employer, or if it's on your conscience, then you can easily add a few lines in bold italics to explain matters.

Consider these examples:

On leaving school I joined the Merchant Navy as a chef and later worked as a chef in restaurants in London before switching careers to sales and marketing.

Prior to becoming a trainer, I enjoyed a successful commercial career in banking and finance followed by a spell as export manager with a trading firm.

It is up to the recruiter to accept you at face value, invite you for an interview, and then delve into your past history if it is deemed relevant. Whatever your age, if you have the background and experience, then there is no reason why you should not be a valid candidate.

Including ancient, irrelevant working history can rule you out from the outset, so don't jeopardise your chances in this manner.

CHAPTER 11

COMPLETING THE PICTURE

We're almost there. All we need to do is include some essential information under a series of headings. These would normally be:

- Education
- Qualifications
- Professional Affiliations
- Computer Skills
- Interests

Others might include:

- Additional Qualifications
- Further Training & Development
- References
- Awards
- Highlights
- Community Involvement
- Volunteer Work

You might have other attributes which would make you more appealing to the reader, so feel free to add more headings as you think appropriate.

Let's look at some of these in more detail.

1. Education & Qualifications

Generally speaking, unless you have only recently left school, your schooling is not important. Employers are much more interested in further education, such as acquiring certificates, diplomas and degrees.

Sometimes, your qualification is directly related to an educational institution (e.g. a degree), so these two headings can be combined. If a qualification has been achieved over a number of years, e.g. chartered accountancy, then list it separately.

2. Computer Skills

Nowadays these are all important, so include them, even if it's simply 'Internet and Email'. It is up to the potential employer to test your proficiency, so there is no need to include your level of competency unless specifically requested.

Computer gaming is an interesting topic nowadays. Whilst the more old-fashioned individuals might see this as a complete waste of time, recent thinking suggests that gamers have critical reasoning and problem solving skills which might be useful to an employer. So if you're a gamer, decide whether it's relevant to the job for which you are applying.

Social networking activities such as Facebook and Twitter are probably best avoided, as they imply that you might waste time during the working day keeping in touch with your friends. That's an expense your employer doesn't want. However, if you can make a case for building a business presence through these sites then by all means include them.

3. Interests

These are often used by an interviewer to break the ice at the start of an interview. It helps to get the interviewee relaxed. Occasionally you might strike lucky if the interviewer has the same interests. Beware of including interests which might give the wrong impression, such as 'socialising' and 'watching movies'. On the other hand, 'distance running' conveys an image of someone who is disciplined, committed and fit.

4. Additional Qualifications

Include these only if they are relevant and add value to your application. A part-time course in massage, which you did for fun and for which you acquired a certificate, might not enhance your chances.

5. References

You are not obliged to divulge any references until the employer is genuinely interested in recruiting you. Even then, it is up to you, as a courtesy, to notify your referees that they can expect a call from a potential employer and the reason for that call. You would not wish to upset your referees if they are called without any advance notice.

Therefore it is inappropriate to include the names of any referees in the early stages of a recruitment exercise, unless specifically asked, as sometimes happens in the public sector. At least that gives you plenty of time to notify your referees.

Should you decide to use 'Referees' as a heading, then 'Available upon request' is the best text to use.

6. Awards or Highlights

If you were a member of a party which climbed Mt. Everest ten years ago, if you won a Rhodes Scholarship, or if you were Head Boy or Head Girl at school, then these are significant achievements and major events in your life. Make them stand out under a separate heading and consider including them on the front page directly underneath the areas of expertise or skills and attributes.

7. Volunteer Work or Community Involvement

Significant in that such work displays a level of unselfishness and a commitment to others perhaps less fortunate. This might be the next to last item on your résumé but it could be the one that actually secures you the job over the other applicants.

In Appendix C you will find plenty of sample résumés in which you can see how information under these headings can be laid out.

CHAPTER 12

ADDING A SMILE TO YOUR RÉSUMÉ

Does humour work? I like to think so.

Sifting through a pile of résumés can be tedious work, so a few words of fun could make all the difference to your chances of securing that interview. The employer might have stressed that theirs is a fun workplace, so why not incorporate some fun in your résumé?

It's your call. You have to weigh things up and decide whether it's appropriate and at what level. It could just be a couple of words, it could be a sentence, or it might be in the heading. If you've had no luck with your existing résumé, then it's worth a try. You have nothing to lose.

How do we achieve this? It's all about using your imagination.

Consider these headings:

ADMINISTRATION OFFICER
Simply the best – well, almost!

SALES EXECUTIVE
Sore knuckles from knocking on doors!
No barrier too big

An opening line can set the right tone:

You probably read about my redundancy (along with 600 others) in the newspaper. It was nice to be famous briefly.

My immediate challenge, apart from getting my husband to put the toilet seat down, is to find a new job.

Taking things further, you can use some very different skills and attributes such as ZANY, QUIRKY, PURE GENIUS, TOP BLOKE, or OFF-THE-PLANET.

In most cases, you'll bring a smile to the reader. Being different could count in your favour, but think carefully before resorting to humour.

CHAPTER 13

BUT WHAT IF?

No matter how good your résumé is, sometimes it just won't work. This might be due to age or other types of discrimination, or simply that you're in the wrong place at the wrong time. Economic downturns affect different areas and sectors of the economy in all sorts of ways.

Some years ago I was introduced to a couple who had two young children and had lost everything. They had gone bankrupt. Both were qualified people in their respective fields. They both had something to offer. They were unlucky, as unforeseen circumstances had caused their business to fail, the one which had been so promising and into which they had ploughed all their assets.

I remember the husband saying to me, "There was a time when the only worry I had was the fact that one of the 18 speakers in my BMW wasn't working." Not surprisingly he was depressed and, like most men under such pressure, had gone into a shell from which it was difficult to extract himself.

During my own working history there have been times when I've faced periods of unemployment but I've usually managed to find a way out of my predicament, even though on occasion I've had to step backwards and accept menial tasks in order to move forwards.

A lot comes down to self-esteem. This individual had lost everything so he needed to start re-building his esteem. I suggested to him that he needed to find any kind of employment, and that a good way of going about this would be to design a flyer. I came up with something similar to the following:

JOB WANTED

PART-TIME, FULL-TIME OR CASUAL

Skills you acquire:

SALES	MARKETING	ADMINISTRATION
COMPUTERS	HUMAN RESOURCES	PLANNING
TRAINING	CUSTOMER SERVICE	RESEARCH

Which leads to:

- Increased sales
- Greater efficiency
- Improved market presence
- Better systems
- & much more

What I achieve:

The chance to apply my considerable knowledge, skills and experience to help your company, whatever its size, set and achieve its goals, maximise its potential, serve its customers, and attain complete job satisfaction for its staff.

The next step:

Contact Martin Darke on (xx) xxxx xxxx or email martindarke@abcnet.com

I then suggested to him that he put on his best suit, go down to his local railway station during rush hour on a working day, and hand out this flyer to the commuters. By doing so he would be demonstrating initiative and, since all those commuters would be heading into town to their respective companies and organisations, one or more might take an interest, call him, and invite him in for a chat.

Had I been in the same city as him I would almost certainly have gone with him on this expedition to give him confidence, but I wasn't, and he didn't follow my suggestion.

I'm happy to say that he did eventually resurrect his career, in a related field to his expertise, but the whole exercise gave me much food for thought and I have often presented this idea to groups of unemployed people.

Even better, I am now using this process with some success in my work helping people with disabilities to find employment. These are individuals whose résumés don't give them much of a chance in a competitive job environment but, by knocking on doors and presenting themselves in front of potential employers, they are tapping in to the hidden job market, demonstrating initiative, creating a very favourable impression and creating opportunities for themselves.

In many companies there are lots of little pockets of work that need doing but nobody to do them. These are not necessarily full-time jobs, but most likely part-time roles. You could easily acquire two or three of these roles which would add up to a full working week.

I know this approach works, because I even used it for myself, finding a new full-time job at the age of 56 with the following poster.

So, if your résumé isn't working for one reason or another, then try this alternative.

PIN THIS ON YOUR WALL

A fit bloke looking for WORK!
mature

Available casual, part-time or full-time

There's lots of things that need doing out there, but businesses don't have the resources or time. It might be:

- office work, such as filing or database entry
- research and marketing
- or just plain, hard YAKKA!

I've got a lot of skills and experience across different sectors, so I've got much to offer, including:

Customer Service	Computers	Databases
Marketing	Training	Recruitment
Research	Proofreading	Driving
Stocktaking	Website Maintenance	Filing

& MUCH MORE!

I've also got the right **ATTITUDE**. I believe in doing a job properly and well. Even better, I've got my own ABN, so you'll get no add-ons such as super, just a plain old invoice.

SO, IF YOU'VE GOT SOME WORK TO BE DONE AND NOBODY TO DO IT, WHY NOT GIVE ME A CALL?
Martin on xxxx xxx xxx or (xx) xxxx xxxx
NOTHING VENTURED, NOTHING GAINED!

CHAPTER 14

COVER LETTERS

One of the advantages of the 30-second impact résumé is that it also acts as a cover letter because it tells the full story.

Unless recruiters or employers specifically ask for a detailed cover letter, they will always turn to the résumés of applicants to determine which ones to interview. In other words they will compare résumés rather than cover letters.

The only instances when cover letters become relevant are;

a)   when an employer asks the candidates to address selection criteria or

b)   when the employer poses a specific issue to candidates to determine whether or not they can actually write a cover letter, for instance school leavers being asked why they are the most suitable person for the job.

However, when applying online, it is easy to give the impression of laziness by not attaching a cover letter. The potential employer might think you are spreading the net as wide as possible, spending as little time as possible on the application, taking a shotgun approach to your job search.

So, whilst your new résumé fulfils the function of being a cover letter, it is perhaps best to write a simple one expressing your interest in the role and referring the reader to your attached résumé.

There is no need to repeat what's already in your résumé, though you might like to emphasise, in the form of bullet points, items raised in job advertisements which might not be covered by your résumé. Examples might include:

- being available on call at weekends
- willingness to travel extensively throughout the region

Bear in mind though that simple adjustments to your qualifying descriptors at the top of your résumé can easily incorporate these items and create the right impression without the need to include them in a cover letter.

APPENDIX A

GLOSSARY

Below is a list of terms to be used either as areas of expertise or skills and attributes. This list is by no means exhaustive. Note too that you can combine some of them, for instance 'Sales & Marketing' and 'Coach & Mentor'.

Accounting
Accounts
Accounts Payable
Accounts Receivable
Acquisitions
Adaptable
Administration
Advertising
Advocacy
Archives
Audio Typing
Auditing
Author
Analysis
Assessment
Banking
Bilingual
Bookkeeping
Budgeting
Building Relationships
Business Development
Campaigns
Catalogues
Change Management

Client Liaison
Coach
Coaching
Commissioning
Committed
Communications
Company Secretary
Competitive
Compliance
Computer Literacy
Computer Modelling
Consulting
Contracts
Corporate Finance
Corporate Governance
Correspondence
Costing
Counselling
Creative
Credit Administration
Credit Analysis
Customer Relationships
Customer Service
Data Entry

Database Management
Dedicated
Design
Detail Conscious
Determined
Diary Management
Disaster Recovery
Displays
Documentation
Due Diligence
E-Commerce
Editing
Event Planning
Exhibitions
Expert Witness
Fast Learning
Feasibility Studies
Filing
Financial Accounting
Forecasting
Group Facilitation
Group Accounting
GST Implementation
Handyman
Hardworking
Human Resources
Inductions
Information Management
Innovative
Investment Analysis
Invoicing
IT Systems
Journalism
Knowledge Management
Languages
Leadership

Lending
Liquidations
Logistics
Mail
Mailing
Maintenance
Management
Management Accounting
Manager
Market Research
Marketing
Media Relations
Mediation
Mentor
Mentoring
Mergers & Acquisitions
Motivator
Negotiations
Network Integration
Networking
Occupational Health & Safety
Office Management
Operations
Operations Management
Organisational Development
Organising
Packaging
Payroll
Petty Cash
Planning
Policy
Presentations
Problem Solving
Procedures
Process Improvement
Procurement

Product Development
Production Management
Profit & Loss
Programming
Project Accounting
Project Management
Promotions
Proofreading
Public Relations
Public Speaking
Publicity
Publications
Purchasing
Quality
Quality Control
Receiverships
Reception
Reconciliation
Records Management
Recruitment
Report Writing
Reporting
Research
Research & Development
Restructuring
Risk Assessment
Sales
Secretarial
Security

Self-Confident
Sense of Humour
Service
Shipping
Sourcing
Stock Control
Strategic Planning
Supervision
Supply & Logistics
Support
Switchboard
Systems Analysis
Systems Development
Systems Management
Systems Review
Taxation
Teaching
Team Player
Teambuilding
Tenders
Testing
Time Management
Training
Training & Development
Transport
Treasury
Troubleshooting
Versatile
Writing

APPENDIX B
ACTION VERBS

Language is very important when describing your achievements. Some verbs are much more powerful than others in getting the message across. Here's a list of some good and not so good (e.g. participated, assisted), action verbs for you to use.

Achieved
Administered
Analysed
Appraised
Approved
Assessed
Assisted
Attained
Attracted
Authorised
Check
Collate
Control
Coordinate
Defined
Delivered
Determined
Developed
Directed
Distributed
Enabled
Ensured
Established
Evaluated
Forecasted
Gained acceptance for
Gathered
Identified
Implemented
Improved
Increased
Installed

Interpreted
Issued
Judged
Justified
Liaised
Limited
Maintained
Managed
Monitored
Obtained
Operated
Participated
Performed
Planned
Prepared
Presented
Processed
Produced
Progressed
Proposed
Provided
Recommended
Reconciled
Reviewed
Set
Specified
Standardised
Submitted
Supervised
Supplied
Supported

APPENDIX C

THE FINISHED PRODUCT

Over the following pages are various examples of résumés which incorporate all of the features we've described to help us create our own high-impact résumé, the one with the 30-second impact designed to get you the interview.

These examples range from students and apprentices looking for their first job to office generalists and professionals such as lawyers and engineers.

This style of résumé works for everyone. Don't be put off if your own profession is not featured. With a little bit of thought and creativity, and possibly a little help from respected friends and relatives, you will soon produce a document which markets you in the best light, one which makes you feel good about yourself.

Don't hold back. Go for it and good luck in your NEW job search!

On page 10, Chapter 3, I wrote that your new résumé should be no more than two pages. From the examples that follow you might get the impression I have broken my rule. Not so!

The size of the pages in this book imposes a few constraints. Examples 1, 3, 4 and 7 are in fact one-page résumés, and the remainder are no more than two pages.

*Formatting your new résumé can be a headache, so I would be more than happy to send you a template to get you started. All you have to do is send me a message via my website at **www.a-new-career-direction.com**.*

Note that certain items have been erased or amended to protect the privacy of individuals. In all cases the name of the author has been used.

EXAMPLE 1

MARTIN DARKE
2 xxxxxxx xxxx, xxxxxxxxxx WA xxxx

Phone: (Home) (xx) xxxx xxxx Mobile: xxxx xxx xxx Email: xxxxxx@hotmail.com

---

CHEMICAL ENGINEERING STUDENT
Looking for work experience in my field
Strong work ethic, great computer skills, a real team player
Available full-time or part-time

Engineering is my passion. I've just completed my first year of study at XXXXXXXXXX University and it's proving to be everything I wanted it to be. In planning my future, I'm now keen to get some genuine work experience in an engineering environment. This will enable me to make an immediate contribution when I eventually graduate, apart from building my confidence, understanding and knowledge. In return for the opportunity, you will get someone who is hard working, totally committed, keen to learn, and willing to take on any role you require. Try me – you won't regret it!

SKILLS & ATTRIBUTES

RESEARCH & ANALYSIS	CUSTOMER SERVICE	ADMINISTRATION
COMPUTER LITERACY	RECEPTION	SECRETARIAL
DATA ENTRY	FILING & MA LING	INVOICING

WORK EXPERIENCE

SECRETARY (CASUAL)　　　　　　　　　　　Dec 2004 - Present
XXXXXXXXXX, Subiaco Campus

Well known college providing a range of educational courses.
- Telephone queries, enrolments and data entry
- Filing, mailing, and general secretarial duties using keyboard and computer skills

55

CLERICAL ASSISTANT
XXXXXXXXXX, West Perth

Dec 2003 – Feb 2004

Oil and gas engineering firm.
- Invoicing, payments and data entry
- General office duties as required

EDUCATION

XXXXXXXXXX University, First Year Chemical Engineering

Units studied as follows:
Engineering Mathematics
Engineering Materials
Engineering Computing
Electrical Systems
Engineering Mechanics
Engineering Professional Studies
Engineering Communications
Brewing & Winemaking Technology

COMPUTER SKILLS

Internet, Email, Word, Excel, various in-house systems

VOLUNTEER WORK

Cerebral Palsy Association - holiday care program for children
Edmund Rice Camp for Kids
Umpire junior school hockey matches
Ronald McDonald House – provide dinner once a month for families of children with cancer

REFEREES

Available upon request

EXAMPLE 2

MARTIN DARKE

23 xxxxx xxxxx, xxxxxxx xxxxxx, London EC1M 6DT

Phone: (Home) xxxxx xxxxxxx   (Mobile) xxxx xxx xxx   Email: xxxxxxx@gmail.com

SPANISH GRADUATE WITH COMMERCIAL INSTINCT
Seeking an entry-level position in investment banking
Well travelled, confident and client-focused

Spanish has always been my passion. My year in Mexico, which gave me exposure to emerging markets and international finance, linked to my vacation work in branding and recent internship with a major law firm, has fermented my interest in commerce, particularly banking and finance. So my ambition is to utilise my strengths in this sector, and to emphasise the point I've just completed a relevant diploma in business and economics. It goes without saying that I have a strong work ethic, and I recognise that I have a great deal to learn before proving my worth.

SKILLS & ATTRIBUTES

CUSTOMER SERVICE	BUILDING RELATIONSHIPS	RESEARCH & ANALYSIS
MARKETING	NEGOTIATIONS	ADMINISTRATION
TEAM PLAYER	COMPUTER LITERACY	TIME MANAGEMENT

HIGHLIGHT
Universidad de las Américas, Puebla, México 2003-4
Study year abroad teaching and assessing modules in Advanced Spanish Language,
American Markets, International Finance and Mexican Civilisation

WORK EXPERIENCE

BUSINESS DEVELOPMENT ADVISER –
BANKING & FINANCE (INTERNSHIP) XXXXX, London   Sep 2005 to Dec 2005

XXXXX is a top-ten City law firm with almost 50 clients from the FTSE 350, and with extensive operations in Central & Eastern Europe. CMS is an alliance of European law firms.
- Business developer for the European network, liaising with committee members across Europe to derive common client bases, e.g. Commerzbank, WestLB and Bank of Austria
- Attend committee conference calls to discuss trends and strategy, having previously conducted research and distributed findings
- Compose marketing material, the end product being used as sales tools by member firms
- Establish and maintain database and records of all activities

ACCOUNTS ASSISTANT   Feb 2001
CENTRO de TURISMO, Tarragona, Spain

A flourishing state-owned tourist and tour guide centre, based in this ancient Roman city. This was a school holiday assignment achieved as a result of high grades and recommendations by my teachers.

- Gained experience of the financial management of small to medium-sized companies, supporting the Chief Financial Officer
- Developed a solid awareness of culturally sensitive issues, as well as the use of the language

BRAND MANAGER SUPPORT (VACATIONS ONLY)   Jun 1999 to Present
XXXXXXXXXX, Manchester

A brand management consultancy established and operated by two widely experienced and highly successful advertising executives. Originally appointed through attending a careers fair at which I impressed the principals.

- Completed a comprehensive investigation of petrol station presentation and branding throughout the United Kingdom, to support the recommendations to the Total Group for re-aligning their brand image
- Received critical acclaim from the consultancy's CEO for my efforts on the above project
- Derived valuable understanding of business processes and behaviour, enhancing my reasoning and analysis skills

EDUCATION

LEEDS UNIVERSITY   2001-5
BA (Hons) Spanish & Geography, Class 2:1
THE GRANGE GRAMMAR 6th FORM, Hartford, Cheshire   1999-2001
4 'A' Levels
Appointed Senior House Captain, responsible for motivating and organising up to 250 pupils

OTHER QUALIFICATIONS

SPANISH CHAMBER OF COMMERCE   2005
Diploma in Spanish for Business & Economics (Credit)

COMPUTER SKILLS

Microsoft Office, Internet & Email

INTERESTS

International markets, overseas travel, sport - mainly cricket, golf and football. (Was Committee Member of Leeds University Cricket Club, responsible for organising kit sponsorship and maintaining the accounts)

 **EXAMPLE 3**

MARTIN DARKE
19 xxxxx xxxx, Mandurah WA 6210
Phone: (Home) (xx) xxxx xxxx   (Mobile) xxxx xxx xxx

HEAVY-DUTY DIESEL MECHANIC
Newly qualified, young, fit, and keen to learn

Diesel mechanics are in my blood and I like nothing more than to take machines apart, fix problems, and service equipment so that it runs as efficiently and smoothly as possible. After making an impression with XXXXXXXXXX through work experience at school, I was fortunate enough to have the opportunity to undertake my apprenticeship with them. I have thoroughly enjoyed the past four-and-a-half years, the last six months of which have been spent working full-time as a tradesman for XXXXXXXXX, on the road and fixing trucks and machinery on site. I'm now ready to expand my horizons, in particular to the construction and mining sectors. I know that I still have a lot to learn but you will find me hardworking, enthusiastic and always ready to meet challenges.

AREAS OF EXPERTISE

EARTHMOVING EQUIPMENT	TRUCKS & CRANES	PREVENTIVE MAINTENANCE
SERVICE & REPAIR	COMPUTERISED DIAGNOSIS	ANALYSIS
CUSTOMER SERVICE	BUILDING RELATIONSHIPS	QUALITY CONTROL

HIGHLIGHT
Apprentice of the Year Award xxxx

PROFESSIONAL EXPERIENCE

DIESEL MECHANIC (CONTRACTOR)   2001 to Present
XXXXXXXXXX CONTRACTING, Waroona

Apprenticed to this firm, a market leader in servicing trucks and earthmoving equipment in WA, through the Chamber of Commerce & Industry.
- Completed my apprenticeship in December, 2004 (block release from Swan TAFE)
- Acquired thorough knowledge of trucks (e.g. MACK) and earthmoving equipment (e.g. Caterpillar, Kohmatsu)
- Now employed as a contractor repairing breakdowns and performing machine maintenance on site

PROFESSIONAL QUALIFICATIONS

SWAN TAFE, Thornlie Campus   2004
Engineering Tradesperson (Automotive)

LICENCES

HR Class (almost complete)
Forklift ticket

OTHER QUALIFICATIONS

Marcsta Safety Course
St John's Ambulance First Aid
Approved Tagging Course

EXAMPLE 4

MARTIN DARKE
24 xxxxx xxxxxx, xxxxxx WA 6028
Phone: (Home) (xx) xxxx xxxx   Email: xxxxx@bigpond.com.au

OFFICE ALL-ROUNDER
Friendly, lively, great computer skills, a real team player
Available full-time or part-time

Having taken a break after being made redundant (along with many others) by
'Which Bank?', I'm now ready to get back into the workforce, equipped with even
more skills than I had before. I have a strong work ethic and you won't find me
leaving until the job is done. My customer service skills are second to none, and
your customers will always be greeted with a smiling face. I'm loyal and hardworking
and I can't wait to get back into an office environment. Try me – you won't regret it!

SKILLS & ATTRIBUTES

CUSTOMER SERVICE	RECEPTION	SWITCHBOARD
BUILDING RELATIONSHIPS	ADMINISTRATION	INFORMATION MANAGEMENT
COMPUTER LITERACY	CASH-HANDLING	TEAM PLAYER

PROFESSIONAL EXPERIENCE

OPERATIONS CLERK   1989 to 2005
COMMONWEALTH BANK, Perth

The well known retail bank. Commenced as a bank teller dealing directly with
customers and was later promoted to the role of clerk providing full administrative
services.
* Cash-handling, account balancing and customer service
* ATM servicing
* Handling customer complaints to achieve satisfactory outcomes to all parties
* Stock ordering and wages
* Office secretary, report writing and reconciliation

Took a break raising my family

REAL ESTATE AGENT   1983 to 1985
XXXXXXXXXX REAL ESTATE, Perth

Well known agency in this sector.
* Listing and selling properties
* Maintaining rental agreements and inspecting houses

TELEPHONIST   1973 to 1981
XXXXXXXXXX COMPANY, Sydney

Established company with 12 staff drivers.
* Supervised the radio room booking trips for clients
* Staff wages, billing and general day-to-day administration

Prior to 1981 I worked as a telephonist and also lived in Canada for five years.

COMPUTER SKILLS
Internet, Email, Word, various in-house systems

OTHER SKILLS
Certificate III in Medical Administration
First Aid

EXAMPLE 5

MARTIN DARKE

8 xxxx xxxx Duncraig WA 6023

Phone: (Home) (xx) xxxx xxxx   (Mobile) xxxx xxx xxx   Email: xxxxxxxx@xxxxxx.org

ADMINISTRATION OFFICER

Bringing order to chaos, with a personal and friendly touch
Setting the standard for others to follow

Diverse experience, from single-handedly setting up and running a backpackers' hostel to counselling drug addicts and ex-offenders to get their lives back on track, has given me the confidence to take on any role involving high expectations from both my employer and its clients. Service delivery and attention to detail are my strengths, to which is added a friendly style backed up by considerable knowledge and understanding of client needs. If you're looking for someone who is committed to getting the job done to the highest standard, then you won't be disappointed.

SKILLS & ATTRIBUTES

CUSTOMER SERVICE	ADMINISTRATION	ACCOUNTING
RECORDS MANAGEMENT	DATA ENTRY	BUILDING RELATIONSHIPS
COMPUTER LITERACY	SYSTEMS	TEAM PLAYER

PROFESSIONAL EXPERIENCE

CONSULTANT   2000 – Present
XXXXXXXX XXXXXXXXXX, Warwick

XXXXXXXX is a member of the Job Network providing a wide range of services to disadvantaged people looking to rejoin the workforce. Commenced in an administration role before being promoted within one year.

- Provide intensive support to long-term unemployed, including drug addicts and ex-offenders
- Liaise with external agencies such as Centrelink, DEWR, employers and training organisations
- Maintain comprehensive computerised records on over 100 cases
- Conduct training courses in career development
- Also work two evenings per week as a telephone counsellor for Salvo Careline (crisis management)

CONTRACTS ADMINISTRATION ASSISTANT (TEMP)   1999
XXXXXXXXXX, Perth

Perth was where I wanted to be and after arriving I found this temporary role for this joint venture managing maintenance contracts for Telstra sites.

- Assisted in the preparation of contracts
- Data entry and general administration including filing

ADMINISTRATOR   1998
XXXXXXXXXX, Sydney
Emigrated to Australia in 1998 and joined this local manufacturer of lenses for the retail optical sector.
- Stock ordering and general administration
- Organised deliveries both interstate and international
- Planned and participated in trade fairs
- Supported sales and marketing team in product launches

RATES & REVENUE OFFICER   1992-1998
XXXXXXXXXX DISTRICT COUNCIL, New Zealand
Local council catering to the needs of up to 500,000 people, a proportion of which were Maori, my interest in which led me to apply for the role.
- Handled all rating enquiries, water billing, and land and building consents
- Researched and resolved complex issues involving Maori affairs

LENDING OFFICER   1992
XXXXXXXXXX, Whangarei
The expiry of the lease on the backpackers' hostel led to a change in career and a role with the third-largest bank in New Zealand.
- Handled all financial transactions for customers in this local branch
- Analysed and approved lending to individuals and small businesses

FOUNDER & MANAGER   1989-1992
XXXXXXXXXX, Whangarei
Identified an opportunity to develop the staff quarters of a well-known resort hotel into a combined facility catering also to the backpacking community.
- Obtained financing to develop and improve the facility, including a new volleyball court
- Operated the hostel single-handedly, utilising backpackers to fulfil functions when required
- Marketed the hostel through tourist organisations
- Learnt to conduct own maintenance on such things as plumbing and vehicles

Prior to establishing the hostel I enjoyed a few years learning the essentials of the hospitality industry, from customer service to administration and accounting.

QUALIFICATIONS

XXXXXXXXXX in-house courses including
Negotiation & Crisis Intervention
Motivational Interviews
Telephone Counselling and Communication

Diploma in Business Studies, Human Resources (planning to resume, partially completed)

ADDITIONAL QUALIFICATIONS

Senior Workplace First Aid Certificate   2002

Certificate IV in Remedial Massage   2004

COMPUTER SKILLS

Internet, Email, Word, Excel, PowerPoint

Various in-house systems and databases

INTERESTS

Outrigger paddling representing XXXXXXXXXX Outrigger Club
Remedial and Swedish massage
Swimming, walking, general fitness

EXAMPLE 6

MARTIN DARKE

8/10 xxxxx xxxxxx, Fawkner VIC 3060

Phone: (Home) (xx) xxxx xxxx   (Mobile) xxxx xxx xxx Email: xxxxxxx@yahoo.com

CREDIT OFFICER, FINANCIAL SERVICES
Specialising in credit and mortgage portfolios
Advanced finance and accounting qualifications

Highly qualified and experienced bilingual (Mandarin & English) lending professional with advanced analytical skills which promote responsible decision-making leading to improved profits. Complete dedication to providing a first-class service, utilising excellent communication abilities to nurture client relationships. Now seeking to utilise my all-round qualifications in finance and accounting for an organisation looking to enhance its presence and image in the financial services sector. Enthusiastic, hardworking and always ready to meet challenges, I describe myself as a person who establishes goals and strives to achieve those goals. Planning is an essential element of my success.

AREAS OF EXPERTISE

CREDIT ADMINISTRATION	CREDIT ANALYSIS	CUSTOMER RELATIONSHIPS
SYSTEMS MANAGEMENT	COMPLIANCE	RESEARCH
RISK MANAGEMENT	TAXATION LAW	CORPORATE FINANCE

PROFESSIONAL EXPERIENCE

CREDIT OFFICER   Aug 2003 to Present
XXXXXXXXXX FINANCIAL GROUP, Melbourne
Established in 1992, headquartered in Sydney, specialising in property related financial services, managing assets of almost $2b and with $450m worth of mortgages on behalf of institutional investors.
- Processing loan applications, ensuring full compliance with policies and procedures
- Developed new systems to improve efficiency
- Regular liaison with brokers, banks, insurance companies and solicitors

FINANCIAL CONSULTANT & SECRETARY (PART-TIME)
XXXXXXXXXX MORTGAGE, Melbourne   Mar 2002 to Jul 2003
Mortgage originator of several major banks with $100m worth of mortgages per annum. Fulfilled this role whilst completing full-time studies.

- Analysed and evaluated loan applications, consistently improving the loan portfolio
- Provided financial advice to clients
- General administration and regular liaison with financial institutions and relevant parties

DEPARTMENT MANAGER   Jul 1999 to Jul 2000
XI'AN HAOTAO ENZYME ENGINEERING Ply. Ltd, Xi'an, China

Attached to the Research Institute for Enzyme Engineering of Shaanxi Academy of Sciences, liaison with sales, suppliers, customers, the Research Institute's needs for product development, product marketing, co-ordinate and implement catalogue production and customer service.

- All external sales, developing customer relationships and building business
- Consistently met required targets and budgets
- Full responsibility for settlement of accounts
- Part of the senior management team, reporting to the Director

PROFESSIONAL QUALIFICATIONS
MIAA Consumer Credit Code (UCCC)
Certificate of Accreditation from Great Pacific Financial Group
Certificate of Accreditation from St. George Bank

EDUCATION & QUALIFICATIONS
Master of Professional Accounting
Victoria University of Technology   2003
Master of Finance
RMIT University 2002
Master of Economics
Northwest University, Xi'an, China   1999
Diploma of English Language
Xi'an Foreign Language University, China   1994

COMPUTER SKILLS
Microsoft Office, Internet, email
MYOB

EXTRACURRICULAR ACTIVITIES & INTERESTS
Secretary of The Chinese Student & Scholar Association, RMIT University
Volunteer assistant of Landmark Education in Melbourne
Jogging, hiking, reading, music and travel

EXAMPLE 7

MARTIN DARKE

14 xxxx xxxxxx, Quinns Rocks WA 6030

Phone: (Home) (xx) xxxx xxxx   (Mobile) xxxx xxx xxx   Email: mdarke@iinet.net.au

QUALIFIED IT TRAINER

Consistently rated as excellent by students
Available on a casual or contract basis

Having had a successful international business career, I have re-invented myself to offer a range of services based on my skills and experience. One of these is computer training for which I have a natural aptitude. In fact, I love it! Following my move to Perth a year ago, I have now become Mission Australia's resident contract IT trainer at their new site in Joondalup. In addition, I provide one-on-one training in people's homes, mainly aimed at the mature-aged market, people who have missed out on computers. My full story can be read at my website www.martindarke.com.au.

SKILLS & ATTRIBUTES

TRAINING	CURRICULUM DEVELOPMENT	GROUP FACILITATION
MARKETING	LECTURING	RÉSUMÉS
CUSTOMER SERVICE	RESEARCH	PROOFREADING

PROFESSIONAL EXPERIENCE

SELF-EMPLOYED   2003 to Present
MARTIN DARKE & ASSOCIATES (ABN 446789624)

Established my own firm to provide a range of services which now include computer training for the mature-unemployed, computer training one-on-one, lecturing, employment workshops for the mature-unemployed, and résumé writing in the private sector.

Current assignments include:
- Resident IT Trainer for Mission Australia at Joondalup delivering courses such as BITES, Certificates I and II in Information Technology, and Intermediate Word and Excel
- Presently developing and writing a new three-day course for Mission Australia which will teach unemployed people how to search for jobs using the internet
- Arrow Computers at Joondalup and Balcatta hand out my flyers to customers requiring PC installation and training

- Provision of IT services to a variety of retained private clients
- Casual lecturing for Challenger TAFE delivering business courses such as Setting up a new small business
- Workshops for the mature-unemployed through Salvation Army Employment Plus

PROFESSIONAL QUALIFICATIONS

SHEFFIELD UNIVERSITY, England
BA (Triple Honours) in Economics, Pure Maths & Stats   1972
SPHERION, Melbourne
Diploma in eBusiness Support (Awarded with Excellence)   2001
NMIT, Melbourne
Certificate IV in Workplace Assessment & Training   2004

EXAMPLE 8

MARTIN DARKE
11 xxxxxxxxx xxxx, Claremont, WA 6010

Phone: (Home) (xx) xxxx xxxx (Mobile) xxxx xxx xxx   Email: xxxxxxxxx@iinet.net.au

COUNSELLING SPECIALIST
Extending my knowledge and experience into career transition
Available part-time or as a contractor

An early career in teaching, specialising in children with disabilities, led to management positions in the public service with a strong emphasis on counselling. I realised this was my vocation, given my natural ability to empathise with people at all levels, allied to my excellent communication and presentation skills. Following a period successfully starting and raising a family, I am about to complete advanced studies in career counselling and am keen to progress in this field with a reputable organisation.

AREAS OF EXPERTISE

COUNSELLING	EDUCATION & TRAINING	GROUP FACILITATION
RESEARCH	CONSULTING	RELATIONSHIP BUILDING
PLANNING	MANAGEMENT	CUSTOMER SERVICE

PROFESSIONAL EXPERIENCE

PRIVATE TUTOR   2002 to Present
STUDENTS WITH DYSLEXIA
Whilst studying and raising my children, I have been working as a specialist tutor in this field.
* devised education programs tailored for the specific needs and interests of individuals
* delivered successful outcomes based on the Hickey Multisensory Language Course

Devoted this period to raising three children, whilst also performing voluntary and community positions relating to local groups and educational institutions.

EEO OFFICER   1990 to 1992
EDUCATION DEPARTMENT OF XX
After completing the Graduate Development Training Program I accepted a role within this Department which itself had some 40,000 staff meeting the education needs of children in Western Australia.

- continuous review of the Department's human resources and employment policies and procedures to ensure compliance with Equal Opportunity legislation
- investigated and managed all EEO complaints including sexual harassment claims
- developed, coordinated and presented training courses for all levels of staff covering EEO legislation and its implications
- instigated and chaired various committees
- prepared recruitment and selection manual as well as a quarterly newsletter

GRADUATE DEVELOPMENT TRAINING PROGRAM,   1989
OFFICE OF EXECUTIVE PERSONNEL
STATE GOVERNMENT OF XXXXXXXXXX

One of 12 participants selected from over 900 applicants for this fast-track program for managerial positions.

Training covered all aspects of management designed to provide participants with a 'Whole of Government' approach to the public service.
- seconded to the Police and Health and Education Departments for several months each, learning on-the-job and conducting research on various projects
- attended numerous professional development courses including Communication Skills, Career Development and Corporate & Financial Management

TEACHER-IN-CHARGE, SPECIAL EDUCATION UNIT   1988
XXXXXXXXXX SENIOR HIGH SCHOOL

Established a new unit for high school students with mild to moderate intellectual and physical disabilities.
- devised and taught programs covering core subjects
- integrated students into mainstream elective subjects
- inducted general teaching staff and assessed both staff and students

TEACHER, YEAR 6   1987
XXXXXXXXXX SCHOOL FOR CHILDREN WITH IMPAIRED HEARING

TEACHER, YEAR 10, HEARING IMPAIRED UNIT   1985 to 1986
XXXXXXXXXX SENIOR HIGH SCHOOL

TEACHER, YEAR 8 &11, HEARING IMPAIRED UNIT   1983 to 1984
XXXXXXXXXX SENIOR HIGH SCHOOL

EDUCATION
UNIVERSITY OF WESTERN AUSTRALIA, Perth
Bachelor of Education   1982

PROFESSIONAL QUALIFICATIONS
EDITH COWAN UNIVERSITY, Perth
Graduate Certificate in Career Counselling   2005 (pending)
(Distinction average mark to date)

PROFESSIONAL AFFILIATIONS
Australian Association of Career Counsellors (pending)
Career Education Association of Western Australia (pending)

COMPUTER SKILLS
Microsoft Office, Pagemaker Desktop Publishing
Internet & Email

EXAMPLE 9

MARTIN DARKE
27 xxxx xxxx, Armadale WA 6112

Phone: (Home) (xx) xxxx xxxx   (Mobile) xxxx xxx xxx   Email: xxxxx@hotmail.com

PIPING SUPERVISOR
Over 20 years' experience in the oil and gas sector
Setting the standard for others to follow

Highly skilled and qualified boilermaker/pipefitter/welder with a thorough knowledge of processes and materials and considerable experience on major projects, both onshore and offshore, ranging from mining sites to platforms and rigs. Conscientiousness, a strong eye for detail, the right work ethic, and good communication skills led to greater responsibility supervising teams on demanding projects. Now available for assignments in which I can apply my skills and knowledge to deliver results to the highest possible standard.

AREAS OF EXPERTISE

SUPERVISOR/ MOTIVATOR	QUALITY ASSURANCE	PLANNING
OH&S	TRACEABILTY	TRAINING & DEVELOPMENT
WORKSHOP SETUP	RECRUITMENT	PROCUREMENT

PROFESSIONAL EXPERIENCE

A serious accident, incurred overseas whilst on holiday, interrupted my career. I have now made a full recovery, benefiting during the rehabilitation process by acquiring more skills and qualifications to enhance my career prospects and add value to future employers.

VARIOUS OFFSHORE ASSIGNMENTS   June 2002 – Aug 2003
CONTRACT EMPLOYERS
A period in which I was able to use my complete range of skills in a variety of locations. Highlights included:
- Welding a 136km 42in-diameter pipeline from Dampier to the North Rankin A platform
- Pipe modifications and general boilermaking and fabrication work on the Jack Ryan Deep Water Drill Ship (largest in the southern hemisphere)
- Modification and customisation work on the Ensco 104 Drill Rig, part of the Bayu Undan Phillips Offshore Project
- Repairs and modifications to the Ensco 56 Offshore Jackup Rig
- Shutdown of the Challis Venture involving work which had to be verified by Lloyds of London
- Coded welder for Ocean Heritage Rig-16E, readying the rig for towing to Singapore

VARIOUS ASSIGNMENTS
CONTRACT EMPLOYERS
1996 to Jun 2002

A period acquiring diverse experience and improving my skills on a range of projects in Western Australia and Queensland. Highlights included

- Structural steel fabrication on vessels and mine shutdowns for Monadelphous, Karratha
- Maintenance of the crushing plant for Nifty Copper Mine near Telfer
- Major shutdown involving pipefitting for the Murrin Murrin Nickel Mine
- Boilermaker/loader operator/maintenance for the Woodside plant at Karratha
- Workshop supervisor (six employees) for Glen Park Engineering, Maddington, specialising in pipework for fuel depots
- Boilermaker for Alcoa, Pinjarra
- Coded welder for HPS St Ives Gold, Kambalda
- Piping of offshore drill rig for Ausclad
- Pipefitter for cooling systems for Austal Ships

VARIOUS
1977 to 1996

Completed my boilermaker apprenticeship in 1981, whilst also doing welding certificates at night school, and began my first job in Sale, Victoria, working on the chimney stacks at the Loy Yang Power Station. Moved to Western Australia in 1988 to continue my career.

PROFESSIONAL QUALIFICATIONS
Boilermaking Trade Certificate   1981
DLI Welding Certificate 1   1981
DLI Welding Certificate 2   1981
Open Gantry Crane   1995
Stick/TIG ASME IX   1998
Elevated Work Platform   1999
Non-Slewing Crane (25 ton) and Open Forklift   1999
OH&S Certificate of Completion (Offshore) – Total Marine Services   2002
Certificate of Completion in Safety Focus 1 – Global SantaFe   2002
SAIPEM (Offshore Pipeline Passo Operator) Qualified Welder   2003

ADDITIONAL QUALIFICATIONS
Swan Maritime Institute Foundation Inc
Certificate IV in Assessment and Workplace Training (BSZ40198)   2004

COMPUTER SKILLS
Internet, Email, Word, Excel

INTERESTS
Rhee Taekwondo (Green Belt) Blue Tip
Riding and rebuilding motorcycles
Fishing and pistol shooting

EXAMPLE 10

MARTIN DARKE
118 xxxx xxxx, xxxxxxxxx WA 6008
Phone: (Home) (xx) xxxx xxxx   (Mobile) xxxx xxx xxx   Email: xxxxxx@aol.com

COMMERCIALLY ASTUTE ADVANCED ENGINEER
Turning ideas into profitable ventures
Enhancing systems to increase efficiency and turnover,
and improve the bottom line

Accomplished and highly qualified mechanical engineer with the ability to take an idea from the design stage, acquire funding for research and development, and manage the project through to production and commercialisation. Particularly adapted to working alongside entrepreneurs in SMEs in developing new products, eventually setting up in-house facilities or outsourcing manufacturing. Recently returned to Perth after a successful spell in the technology transfer division of an academic institution recognised for its achievements in this sector. Now looking to assist Western Australian companies expand their operations and develop domestic and overseas markets.

AREAS OF EXPERTISE

STRATEGIC PLANNING	R&D	SYSTEMS DESIGN
PROJECT MANAGEMENT	FINANCIAL MANAGEMENT	CAE, CAD/CAM
TRAINING AND DEVELOPMENT	MANAGER / MOTIVATOR	TOTAL QUALITY MGMT

PROFESSIONAL EXPERIENCE

MECHANICAL ENGINEERING CONSULTANT, ENTERPRISE EXCHANGE
XXXXXXXXXX, United Kingdom   1997 to 2005
Specialised department devoted to developing key collaborative industrial projects. Highlights included:

- Secured £80k funding and provided technical support to developing a leading child seat for cars
- Submitted bids and obtained funding to develop advanced unmanned vertical take-off and landing craft for defence forces
- Involved in an innovative bike-rental scheme adopted by eight London boroughs
- Participated in the development of a prototype machine which will be utilised to manufacture specialist heat exchangers and chemical reactors
- Gained £130k funding from The Carbon Trust to support innovation in higher efficiency industrial coolers
- Appointed as a London Technology Network Business Fellow to represent the University in all commercial activity

- Contributed to a 16% growth in turnover for a company by developing a management information systems based on radio frequency hand-held terminals
- Identified various system improvements to support the development of an international supply chain for a British tool manufacturer

SENIOR LECTURER   1993 to 1997
UNIVERSITY OF XXXXXXXXXX, United Kingdom
Lectured in CAE and engineering design, whilst also gaining funding for a range of opportunities that enhanced the profile of the department.
- Gained £168k funding for a KTP programme with an engineering SME
- Responsible for technology elements of a successful Brite Euram bid for £750k to improve energy efficiency in domestic swimming pools
- Presentation to the Parliamentary Defence Select Committee in association with McDonnell Douglas on the benefits of high-velocity machining

SENIOR MECHANICAL PROJECT ENGINEER   1989 to 1993
XXXXXXXXXX AEROSPACE, United Kingdom
Description of company.
- Responsible for the project management of jig and tool design and subsequent manufacture for a range of blue-chip companies including Rolls Royce, Dornier and Westland
- Developed high-level company capability in 3D-modelling and CNC machining
- Introduced a sub-contract manufacturing supply chain to support tool procurement

SYSTEMS DEVELOPMENT ENGINEER   1987 to 1989
xxxxxxxxxxxxxxx, United Kingdom
Description of company.
- Primary role to investigate the technical and commercial viability of a wide range of engineering systems and hardware
- Gained Board support for £1m capital investment
- Implemented the MSA purchasing system in technical areas

VARIOUS, PERTH & UNITED KINGDOM   1977 to 1986
Commenced my career as an engineering officer cadet for a cruise shipping line before moving on to two positions in Perth with an engineering consultancy and then Swan Brewery.

QUALIFICATIONS
LIVERPOOL POLYTECHNIC, ENGLAND
MSc (Computer Aided Engineering)   1987
BSc Honours 2:1 (Mechanical Engineering)

PROFESSIONAL AFFILIATIONS
INSTITUTION OF INCORPORATED ENGINEERS, United Kingdom
Member
ADVANCED PROJECT MANAGEMENT GROUP, United Kingdom
Member

COMPUTER SKILLS
MRP/ERP (Alliance, Jobshop)
Various FEA,CFD, 3D-Modelling Systems
Microsoft Project, Procurement Systems
Microsoft Office, Internet, Email

SPECIAL ACHIEVEMENTS
Angle Technology Associate, United Kingdom
Engineering Business Partnership Ambassador, United Kingdom

OTHER QUALIFICATIONS
Football Association Qualified Soccer Coach

EXAMPLE 11

MARTIN DARKE

5 xxxxxxxxx xxxxxx, Footscray, Melbourne 3011

Phone: (Home) xxxx xxxx (Mobile) xxxx xxx xxx Email: xxxxxx@alphalink.com.au

RECORDS & DOCUMENT MANAGEMENT SPECIALIST
Developing, implementing and maintaining best-practice systems

Highly experienced, qualified, and skilled practitioner in this area, having initiated and successfully implemented a complete change-management project in a high-profile public sector organisation. Fully conversant with the latest technologies (including TRIM) in relation to recordkeeping, thorough knowledge of the laws relating to risk and compliance, and proven ability to develop policies and procedures. Excellent listening and communication skills with a natural aptitude to motivate, train and lead staff to provide a service which exceeds expectations. Ready and able to accept greater challenges and responsibilities, and one who thrives in situations demanding change.

AREAS OF EXPERTISE

RECORDS MANAGEMENT	STRATEGIC PLANNING	POLICY & PROCEDURES
RISK ASSESSMENT & COMPLIANCE	BUDGETING	COMMUNICATIONS
PROJECT MANAGEMENT	TRAINING & DEV	DEPARTMENT MGMT

PROFESSIONAL EXPERIENCE

MANAGER, RECORDS & ADMINISTRATIVE SERVICES
XXXXXXXXXX, East Melbourne   Aug 1998 to Present

The XXXXXXXXXX is the peak body for fire and emergency services throughout metropolitan Melbourne comprising up to 500 administrative staff and some 1500 operational staff. Began as a Records Officer, promoted to Acting Manager in April, 1999 and promoted again to Manager in 2003, reporting to the Director of Corporate Governance, assuming full responsibility for the recordkeeping service in this high-profile public sector organisation.

Key achievements and responsibilities include:

• strategised, piloted and successfully implemented, on time and within budget, the XXXXXXXXXX's records management project, involving negotiations across the whole organisation, presentations to the executive management team, and preparation of Board papers. The XXXXXXXXXX has traditionally been resistant to change, adding complexity to the issues and the need to drive and sustain the momentum over a two-year period in order to meet the goals

- next phase of the change-management process, now ready for implementation, is a $1.4 million electronic document and records management system covering multiple sites. Total control of this project from initial understanding of the issues through to planning, budgeting, requesting funding and now a request for tender
- full cost-centre control and allocation to all departments
- created an approved standard and tools for the management of records, including disposal schedule, thesaurus, policy and procedures
- substantially eliminated the corporate legal risk in the recordkeeping area
- established a departmental capability for records management, where none had existed before, recruiting and training a skilled and efficient team, comprising seven permanent and 6-8 contract staff
- liaised with the Public Records Office and other government organisations to ensure the setting of complementary standards
- developed and delivered training on records management procedures and principles
- wrote tender documentation and heavily involved with analysing and selecting external suppliers of software
- introduced quality assurance aimed at ensuring compliance as well as continuous improvement
- member of the Executive Managers Group which is instrumental in identifying potential improvements and putting forward proposals for approval

ARCHIVIST & RECORDS OFFICER   Jul 1997 to Aug 1998
XXXXXXXXXX UNIVERSITIES, Melbourne
Part-time simultaneous roles for these two entities.
- developed an efficient management system for unattached documents
- described and developed a search aid for discrete bodies of records

NURSE   1990 to 1997
XXXXXXXXXX HOSPICE, Melbourne
Hospice providing palliative care to some 100 patients.
- day-to-day nursing in a demanding environment

EDUCATION
Mt ELIZA BUSINESS SCHOOL
Master of Business Administration (Executive Operations)   2005 (commencing)
Graduate Diploma of Business Administration (Executive Operations) 2004 (completion)
Graduate Certificate of Business Administration (Executive Business Operations)   2003

MONASH UNIVERSITY
Graduate Diploma of Archives & Records Management   1996

MELBOURNE COLLEGE OF DIVINITY
Bachelor of Theology   1995

SPECIAL ACHIEVEMENT
Winner of the Sir Rupert Hamer Award for Records Management Excellence

PROFESSIONAL AFFILIATIONS
Australian Society of Archivists
Records Management Association of Australia

COMPUTER SKILLS
Microsoft Office Suite, TRIM, System Software Design & Implementation
Internet & Email

INTERESTS
Ballet, opera, classical music, cycling and reading

EXAMPLE 12

MARTIN DARKE
1 xxxxxx xxxx, NSW 2104, Australia
Phone: (xx) xxxx xxxx Fax: (xx) xxxx xxxx Mobile: xxxx xxx xxx
Email: xxxx@optusnet.com.au

COMMERCIAL LAWYER
Supporting senior executives in resolving complex legal issues
Considerable Asian experience, specialising in financial services

After a successful period in Hong Kong, acquiring expertise in both the public and private sectors, I returned to Australia in 1996 and have devoted the past years to ensuring that my children have a solid foundation for their future, putting my own career development aside for a while. It is now appropriate to rejoin the commercial sector, applying my main strength as an in-house lawyer to helping entrepreneurs and directors drive their businesses forward, particularly those looking to expand overseas.

AREAS OF EXPERTISE

LITIGATION & ADVOCACY	COMPLIANCE	COMMERCIAL DOCUMENTS
RESEARCH & ANALYSIS	PROJECT MANAGEMENT	POLICIES & PROCEDURES
MANAGEMENT/MENTOR	TRAINING AND DEVELOPMENT	AUTHOR/PRESENTER

PROFESSIONAL EXPERIENCE

LEGAL PRACTITIONER
PRIVATE PRACTICE, Sydney   1996 to Present
On returning to Australia I have operated independently as a barrister, at the same time working as a solicitor within a local practice targeting the small business sector and the general public.
- Drawing up commercial agreements for a range of clients and projects
- Criminal prosecutions
- Advising small businesses on setup and future development
- Consultant to a Hong Kong-based securities house implementing a compliance regime

LEGAL DIRECTOR & COMPANY SECRETARY
XXXXXXXXXX FAR EAST Ltd, Hong Kong   May 1994 to May 1996
Asian regional headquarters and wholly owned subsidiary of XXXXX Plc, United Kingdom.
- Establishment and maintenance of a legal/compliance department for Hong Kong and the region
- Policies and procedures for all operations
- Research into regional expansion, specifically India and Vietnam

- Monitoring and advising on sensitive issues such as money laundering activities
- Full responsibility for all commercial contracts and agreements

LEGAL COUNSEL
SECURITIES & FUTURES COMMISSION,
Hong Kong   May 1990 to Apr 1994

In-house counsel for this high-profile agency monitoring the relevant financial markets.
- Prosecuting breaches of the Securities, Commodities Trading and Securities Disclosure of Interests Ordinances
- Advising on proposals concerning legislative changes to all ordinances covering these markets
- Advising the head of the Licensing Department on applications for registrations by persons involved in the business of dealing in securities and the giving of investment advice
- Conducting statutory disciplinary proceedings against persons for misconduct and not being fit and proper.

SENIOR CROWN COUNSEL
ATTORNEY GENERAL'S CHAMBERS, Hong Kong   1983 to 1990

Commenced as Legal Aid Counsel for two years and then promoted to more senior roles.
- Prosecuted complex commercial fraud cases in the District and High Courts, the longest of which proceeded for six months in the High Court
- Prosecuted violent crime, including murders, incest, robbery and drug trafficking in the District and High Courts
- Assisted in the establishment of the Drug Trafficking Recovery of Proceeds Unit in the Attorney General's Chambers
- Gave lectures to law students, police and other enforcement agencies on various aspects of evidence and criminal procedure

LEGAL PRACTITIONER
PRIVATE PRACTICE, Melbourne & Darwin   1977 to 1983

Early career gaining experience across a broad range of legal matters.
- General practice including insolvency, building arbitration, personal injury/ workers' compensation, commercial litigation, trade practices, family law and criminal law
- Plaintiff work for the North Australian Aboriginal Legal Aid Service

EDUCATION
UNIVERSITY OF MELBOURNE
LLB/BA (Economics & Politics) 1976

QUALIFICATIONS
Barrister & Solicitor
NSW, ACT, Victoria and Northern Territory
Barrister
Hong Kong
Solicitor
United Kingdom

PUBLICATIONS
Paper on 'Legal & Regulatory Matters Affecting Stock Markets'
Seminar on Stock Markets
Hanoi & Ho Chi Minh City, Vietnam April 1995

Paper on 'Comparative Regulatory Frameworks of Securities Markets'
Seminar on the Development of Securites Markets
Hanoi, Vietnam July 1995

COMPUTER SKILLS
Microsoft Office, Internet & Email

EXAMPLE 13

MARTIN DARKE
House x, Sea Island, Islands at Old Fort Bay, Nassau,
Bahamas (not for correspondence)
Phone (Res): x-xxx-xxx-xxxx Mobile: x-xxx-xxx-xxxx Email: xxxxx@coralwave.com

TECHNICAL ANALYST & STRATEGIST, GLOBAL MARKETS
One of Asia's leading technical analysts

Over 20 years of experience with leading institutions in the investment sector and now recognised as one of Asia's leading technica analysts. Reputation has been built on solid investment advice, both discretionary and advisory, founded upon detailed research and analysis, continually scrutinised by the investment media. Underlying theme of professionalism, ethics and integrity, resulting in loyal and substantial base of high-net-worth clients. Now returning to Asia to be based in Hong Kong, having acquired additional experience and exposure to North American investment markets and practices.

AREAS OF EXPERTISE

TECHNICAL ANALYSIS	RESEARCH	STRATEGY
CLIENT LIAISON	INVESTMENT MANAGER	DISCRETIONARY TRADING
COMMENTARY	MENTOR	TRAINING & DEVELOPMENT

PROFESSIONAL EXPERIENCE

TECHNICAL STRATEGIST
XXXXXXXXXX MANAGEMENT, Nassau   June 2004 - Present
US$200m hedge fund, established in 1997, investing in global emerging markets and hard assets.
- Generating ideas for the short side of the company's portfolios using technical analysis
- Advice and decision-making on stop levels and profit-taking

REGIONAL TECHNICAL STRATEGIST
XXXX, Hong Kong   1999 - May 2004
Top-ranked Asian broker.
- Rated No.1 technical/quantitative analyst in the AsiaMoney 2003 Survey
- Organised and participated in numerous roadshows and conferences throughout the region
- Frequent appearances as investment specialist on CNN, CNBC and Bloomberg TV
- Cited in a number of internal client surveys

DIRECTOR OF RESEARCH
XXXX SECURITIES   Feb 1995 - 1999
The brokerage arm of this leading global financial institution. Commenced as Regional Technical Analyst and was promoted to Director in June, 1998.
- Ranked as No.1 or 2 technical analyst in most Asian countries by AsiaMoney
- Organised and participated in various roadshows

DIRECTOR
XXXX SECURITIES, Hong Kong   1992 - 1995

MANAGING DIRECTOR
XXXX FUTURES, Hong Kong
Indonesian-backed operation which purchased AMIS to establish its presence.
- Built a substantial client base of high-net-worth individuals
- Achieved annual double-digit growth in brokerage revenues
- Established global network of correspondent brokers

DIRECTOR
XXXXX SERVICES (AMIS), Hong Kong   1987 - 1992
Investment house, owned by the London-based XXXXXXXXXX Group, later taken over by XXXXXXXXXX.
- Recruited as Associate Director and promoted soon afterwards, acquiring minority shareholding
- No. 2 revenue producer throughout whole organisation

FINANCIAL CONSULTANT
XXXX ASIA PACIFIC, Hong Kong   1985 - 1987
Headhunted to join this global institution.
- Member of Falcons Club, a reward for high revenue streams
- Received awards for generating large investment funds from clients

TRADER
XXXXX, London, Hong Kong & Singapore   1976 - 1985
Commencement of career with this old-established trading house which specialised in cocoa.
- Comprehensive training in physical and futures markets, including secondment to Ghana
- Transferred to Hong Kong in 1980 and helped to establish Singapore office

EDUCATION
Northwood School, England
Two 'A' Levels

PROFESSIONAL AFFILIATIONS
Technical Analysis Society of Hong Kong
Founder Member (xxxx) and Chairman (xxxx)

QUALIFICATIONS
Society of Technical Analysts Examination, London   1992
Distinction and the highest pass mark ever achieved in Hong Kong
Securities, Futures and Options Examination, USA 1994

INTERESTS
Soccer, all things Italian

ABOUT THE AUTHOR

Born in Nottingham, Martin Darke graduated from Sheffield University in 1975 with a triple honours degree in economics, pure mathematics and statistics.

Martin's first job was with The Hong Kong & Shanghai Banking Corporation and he was lucky enough to be posted to Hong Kong where he spent three years from 1976-79. His next posting was to Muscat in the Middle East, after which he returned to Hong Kong where he spent the next few years in China trade. He then worked for a Japanese business consultant and had a spell with a commercial investigation agency as finance and administration manager.

In 1988 he was asked to become a recruitment consultant with Ernst & Whinney (later Ernst & Young). He built a strong multinational team which diversified into human resources consulting and had many successes.

After arriving in Australia in 1997 he was made redundant and after short periods with other recruitment firms, knew he had to change career, taking a year off to do a diploma in information technology. He qualified with an award for excellence but was too 'old' for the industry and all the so-called 30,000 vacancies were non-existent. He says his biggest mistake was assuming that there was a full-time job waiting for him. There wasn't.

After meeting Grace Johnston, Martin became aware of the skills he had to offer and built his own business, providing a range of services with the underlying theme of helping people.

In 2010, Martin found a job which was truly meant for him, helping people with disabilities to find employment.